My Life on the Autism Spectrum:

Misunderstandings, Insight & Growth

TRACEY COHEN

Published by Pacelli Publishing
Bellevue, Washington

**My Life on the Autism Spectrum:
Misunderstandings, Insight & Growth**

All rights reserved. No part of this book may be reproduced or transmitted in any form or by any means, electronic or mechanical including photocopying, recording or by any information storage or retrieval system, without the written permission of the publisher, except where permitted by law.

Limit of Liability: While the author and the publisher have used their best efforts in preparing this book, they make no representation or warranties with respect to accuracy or completeness of the content of this book. The advice and strategies contained herein may not be suitable for your situation. Consult with a professional when appropriate.

Cover and interior designed by Pacelli Publishing
Cover and author photos by Martin Wooledge Photography

Copyright © 2020 by Tracey Cohen

Published by Pacelli Publishing
9905 Lake Washington Blvd. NE, #D-103
Bellevue, Washington 98004

Printed in the United States of America

ISBN 10: 1-933750-66-9
ISBN 13: 978-1-933750-66-8

Books by Tracey Cohen

Six Word Lessons on Female Asperger Syndrome: 100 Lessons to Understand and Support Girls and Women with Asperger's

Six-Word Lessons on the Sport of Running: 100 Lessons to Enjoy Running for a Lifetime

Contents

Dedication 6

Introduction 7

Bewilderment and Difficult Relationships 9

Institutionalized as a Preteen 15

Education and Employment:
  Challenges and Achievements 21

My Journey to Diagnosis 29

My Top Six Challenges 35

Running: My Heart and Soul 43

Final Thoughts 49

Best Practices for People with Autism 57

Note from the Author 60

Recommended Resources 61

Dedication

It is all too easy to view people who are different from the norm as unpleasant, annoying or even downright weird. It takes a special person to see past first impressions, challenging behaviors and views different from one's own.

People on the autism spectrum are often assumed to be strange, difficult, aloof.

This book is dedicated to each and every person willing to not only accept our differences but be appreciative, welcoming and ready to learn our viewpoints as well as the ways in which we function best and why this is so.

Thank you to everyone who has extended kindness, shown patience and understanding or is ready to learn just how boring and ineffective our world would be if we were all the same.

Introduction

In the pages that follow, I will entrust you with many intimate details about myself, many of which cause me a great deal of shame and embarrassment. But this is not a self-serving cleansing.

I was born with autism, but my family and I did not even know the word autism, let alone its meaning or that it is part of my essence, until I stumbled upon the information at thirty years of age. Nine years later I was diagnosed with Asperger syndrome, a condition on the autism spectrum.

As I approach my fiftieth birthday, I have found the strength to more openly share my story with a single goal in mind; I wish to help.

I know what it's like to be misunderstood and excluded; to feel alone, confused and awkward and like I do not fit anywhere in the world, including my own family. I understand what it's like to want to truly connect with friends and loved ones but not know how or understand why I am the way I am.

While thankfully there is a great deal more awareness and information about autism than when I was born in 1971, thanks to so many wonderful leaders in the field, I believe information about females and a genuine understanding of the many flavors of autism is still lacking.

I hope to help change this. I strive to help people on the spectrum find the confidence and strength to truly be proud and believe in themselves; to live life fully and unapologetically no matter how similar or different from the norm it may be. I aim to help family, friends and caregivers more fully understand us and our viewpoints, to help them help us and to finally find the connection and peace that we all so wish to have.

I understand that so much of this will resonate with the many different challenges people face, and not one is more difficult than the next. But autism is my reality and I hope to shed light on its truths and help people on and off the spectrum learn that a diagnosis of autism is not a life sentence nor is it something to be mourned or ashamed of. We can all live full happy lives marked with individual goals, learning, achievements, and meaningful connections no matter how many times we fall or what challenges we may face.

Thank you for sharing my journey. I hope by the end of the book you will feel understood, validated, informed, inspired, confident and ready to move forward and never quit no matter how bumpy the road may be at times.

Bewilderment and Difficult Relationships

The signs were there; the information and compassion were not.

From my earliest days born in a world that has always been foreign to my basic intrinsic needs, logic and desires, I have been considered "difficult."

I was not a happy baby. I cried a lot but did not babble; I would not take my bottle or make eye contact and I did not like to be held.

My mother has a vivid memory of my pushing so forcefully to get out of her arms, even as a newborn, that she nearly dropped me on several occasions.

"There was something very different about you from your sister," she recalled, and her innate maternal instincts told her something was not right. But when she tried to share her concerns with medical professionals, family and friends, she was told that she was overreacting, that she was a bad mother, that I had emotional problems, and that I, even as an infant, was a brat.

And so, without any proper guidance or resources to speak of, from my earliest days on earth, there was a lot of miscommunication, pain and incorrect assumptions along the way.

Father - George

My dad and I clashed from the very beginning. He enjoyed showing his affection through rough, physical play and lots of hugs, squeezes and kisses. This approach was a huge success with my sister; not so much for me.

Dad trying to soothe me

Because touch has always affected me adversely, I recoiled from his intended display of affection and instead perceived it as a form of punishment, but for what I did wrong, I could not understand. He also teased, a lot, and unbeknownst to him, I digested the meaning of his words in their most literal sense.

Though I was finally diagnosed with Asperger syndrome in 2009 at the age of thirty-nine, another nine years passed before we had our first genuine conversation about my autism and how it affected him.

"I was frustrated," my father said. "I thought I did something wrong and didn't know how to treat you. Plan B was to keep a distance and react when you asked for something."

While my father's logic is understandable, it left me feeling unloved, confused and deemed a "bad girl," without a clue as to why.

My father also shared that he does not remember my ever asking for affection, so he abided by and lived with what he thought were my wishes. He said though that he still loved me.

Unfortunately, I did not understand that it was my responsibility to ask for displays of love after "Plan A" did not take, nor did I know exactly what I needed or how to express it.

Though our relationship today continues to be strained, learning about autism and being diagnosed has slowly helped to improve things.

"There's no doubt in my mind," my father maintains regarding my diagnosis, "it explains a lot."

Sister - Michelle

Photo by Santa Fabio

"I never hated you," my sister, Michelle, older by three years, insists. "I don't know why you think that."

While Michelle remembers initial excitement about having a baby sister, jealousy quickly followed.

"I think it started when I lost something in the cushion and Mom couldn't help."

Whether she was feeding me, changing my diaper or taking care of any number of the demanding needs of a newborn infant, it is no surprise that three-year-old Michelle could not understand why Mom was no longer available for her own immediate needs. Unfortunately, as a sensitive person, even as a baby, I soon felt and internalized her resentment.

Michelle and me at 5 and 2

Michelle's teasing also affected me greatly. "It's just my nature, I'm a teaser," she explained. "It was intended to be playful. However, I think that as a child, I took it too far. I don't remember teasing you because I hated you or to make you feel bad. I'm sure there were times I wanted to make you feel bad because I do know that we fought, but maybe I was also trying to get a reaction from you because you liked to be by yourself."

Though she couldn't have known, I felt tormented. I have always been easily overwhelmed in any social situation including what to most would be considered basic family interactions. I believe the teasing caused me to withdraw even more as a means of self-preservation.

"There was no natural warmth," Michelle added. "You would stiffen whenever I went to hug you; I felt rejected."

Unfortunately, I did not have the awareness or communication skills to explain that my reaction was involuntary, a protective instinct due to my tactile sensory difficulties. And though I continually try and wish so many things were different, this is not something that I have been able to change.

"If our generation grew up with the integration and understanding that is available to families today, I believe things would have been different between us," Michelle acknowledged. "Unfortunately, I did not know."

Mother – Joan

Mom at her wedding

Post-race relaxation with Mom, my personal "cheerleader."

Despite her feelings of inadequacy due to what she perceived to be my rejection of her nurturing efforts, my mom has never stopped trying to show her love for me and has always been my biggest supporter. Left confused by the dismissive reactions she received from professionals and family members regarding her concerns for my wellbeing, she knew in her heart that I was not going through a "stage" and would not outgrow whatever it was that set me apart from the normalcy of my sister. Having no one else to turn to for guidance and support, she acquiesced with the recommendations given to her by those she felt had "more experience and knew better."

"I realize now that my reactions towards you only made things worse," my mom sadly acknowledged in one of our many post-autism diagnosis conversations. "I was always correcting you rather than being open to your views and ways of doing things and allowing you be an individual and develop your own style. I believe this led to your being afraid of making mistakes."

"Families are supposed to be supportive and kind," she continued. "We were the opposite of that for you. Michelle and Dad teased you relentlessly, and though I knew so much was being misinterpreted, I never did anything about it."

My mom also remembers that as I got older I rejected any efforts of closeness and continually pushed people away.

"If something went wrong or there was a difficult situation, you wouldn't ask for help, and if we found out and asked why you hadn't told us, you would only express that you wanted to be a good girl. I remember how you got lost walking back from a friend's house when you were in elementary school. You eventually made it home, but you wouldn't talk about it or let anyone help and you did not cry."

For my part, the pain, confusion and discontent that I have caused pains me deeply, and while there is no eliminating the past, I am constantly working hard to repair relationships and hope to create a better present and future for our world at large, even in the smallest of ways.

Institutionalized as a Preteen

I was diagnosed with anorexia nervosa when I was eleven years old. But let's step back bit.

Keeping in mind that my autism was never detected by professionals until I sought diagnosis at age thirty-nine, I experienced a life-altering doctor visit when I was all of six years old.

Always a slight child and picky eater, these qualities were exacerbated around the time I was five due to a minor urinary tract problem. After undergoing a small surgical procedure, my appetite improved, and I started eating better. At my yearly physical when I was six, the doctor noticed that I had gained ten pounds. She immediately reprimanded me and said, "You can't keep gaining weight this way, you're getting fat."

At my sixth birthday party, shortly before the doctor told me I was "getting fat."

My mom vows that I was nowhere near being overweight. Having been a young child, I do not clearly remember how I genuinely looked or what my body mass index might have been, but I do remember feeling humiliated and being so upset that I vomited in her office.

Throughout my childhood for as long as I can remember, my mom, dad and sister struggled with their weight and were perpetually dieting. The same was true for many of my aunts, uncles, grandparents and cousins. In addition, I grew up in the 1970s when "thin was in." Television airwaves were flooded with commercials about diet, exercise, weight loss and food, all showing a thinner body type, especially for females, as ideal and a means of being beautiful, loved and successful.

My mom very clearly remembers how from the time I began to talk, around age two I "expressed an awareness and aversion to people who were fat." She described an incident at the grocery store when I was not even three years old.

"You were sitting in the cart when we were in the checkout lane and a heavyset woman got in line behind us. You looked at her and asked, 'Why are you so fat?'"

While most assumed that I was being rude and bratty, I truly meant no harm. I was only being inquisitive, a quality that has never diminished despite the mixed reactions I have received over the years.

"After the incident at the doctor's office," my mom continued, "you became more and more preoccupied about weight and fat, and I knew that you were taking what you heard on TV as a rule, but I didn't know what to do. Every professional I spoke with told me that I was the problem."

Perpetuated by the doctor visit and amplified by teasing about my maturing body from family members and bullies I encountered on my walk to and from school, I remember trying to put myself on a diet. Innately literal and having no concept of change, my plan made complete logistical sense. My doctor, the highest authority in my understanding, told me I was fat; the people on TV substantiated that fat was bad; my own family showed me that fat people should go on diets and lose weight. The lower the number on the scale, the better the reward, including being accepted and loved, sentiments I so desperately sought. Unfortunately, I never heard the ads on TV or people on diets speak of a stopping point, only that losing weight and lower scale readings were best.

As my rigid temperament increased and my weight decreased, my parents eventually took me to see a child psychiatrist. Rather than connecting my rigidity, resistance to change and literal mindset to autism, the psychiatrist assumed I was seeking control and attention. As my weight tumbled down and I refused to acknowledge anything I knew to be untrue or that varied from what I had already been told, the psychiatrist ultimately decided that he could no longer treat me on an outpatient basis and convinced my parents to send me to an institution. I was eleven years old.

I will never forget that first day and the terror I felt being cast into the unknown; left in an unfamiliar environment with all kinds of strangers, staff and patients, whose behaviors were foreign, confusing and downright intimidating.

And then there was the noise. The thunderous slam of the doors, not unlike that of a jail cell, which coursed through my body, piercing my very core every time they slammed shut, sealing my fate on "The Unit," leaving me doubtful that I would ever be released or see my family again.

Huddled in a corner, I was left alone to sob for hours until one of the older and larger patients came to soothe and take me under her wing.

The noise level of my environment never decreased and further escalated when children exhibited threatening and harmful behavior, requiring staff to restrain their outbursts and muscle them to what was referred to as the "QR" or padded Quiet Room. But I eventually resigned myself to my situation. The days had a semblance of routine consisting of self-care, school, therapy and scheduled activities, and I found ways to cope and fend for myself when my "friend," who struggled with schizophrenia, was carted off to the QR.

I was typically seen by the psychiatrist twice each week, but unfortunately, other than increases in my weight, no real progress was made. I remember how the doctor insisted I was being controlling and seeking attention when in reality I was scared, trying to be a "good girl" and just wanted to be left alone. I found his attitude, along with most of the staff who watched over us day and night, to be cool, judgmental and condescending. As a result, I became even more mistrustful of family, doctors and people in general.

Some of the patients encouraged me to engage in destructive behaviors. They also shared secrets of devastating horrors inflicted upon them.

One teen who was also institutionalized for anorexia and had been in and out of institutions for years, tried to teach me to lie, hide food and explained how to regurgitate meals we were forced to eat. Others gave me my very first lessons in sex education. They boasted in detail about their erotic sexual exploits and explained the meanings of sexual slang, teasing me for my naivete. A few gentle souls expressed very matter-of-factly how various relatives and family friends had forced them to engage in heinous sex acts and made terrifying threats to them if the behaviors were reported.

I grew up quickly and never spoke of the things I learned.

"When you were being treated by the doctor, I knew you were just biding time rather than the treatment making a difference," my mom lamented. "I felt it but did not know how disastrously the whole experience impacted the Asperger syndrome which every professional treating you apparently had no knowledge of and/or let go unrecognized."

This is during my time at the institution, when I was granted an overnight stay at home for my Bat Mitzvah. I missed my dog, Samantha, terribly and she was a great comfort to me.

I eventually earned day and subsequent weekend visits with my family, but these reunions were awkward and engulfed with friction, especially with my mom, who took on the brunt of food preparation and enforcement, precisely following the guidelines implemented in the institution. I felt betrayed and even more of an outsider than before I was sent away.

As the months dragged on and my weight plateaued and no other progress was made, I was eventually released after about a year. My weight quickly plummeted again, and I was sent back after a few short months. My second institutionalization was much of the same if slightly longer. But this time when I was released, shortly before the start of my sophomore year of high school, I was clear on the parameters for staying out of the institution.

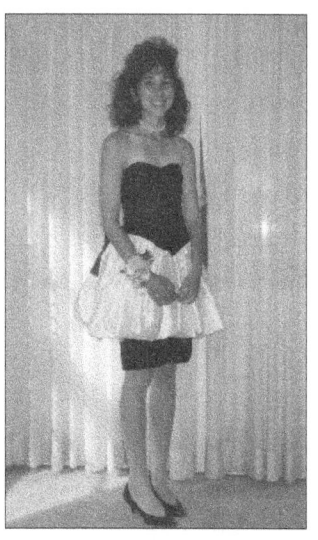

After my release, I slowly adjusted and even earned my driver's license and was asked to a few high school dances.

Despite the countless therapy sessions and observations by numerous professionals, my autism remained hidden, leaving me to my own devices. Determined to survive, over the years I have developed strategies to cope with my autism and learn and maintain healthy eating habits. It's an ongoing process with many falls along the way, but I do my best each day and try to adjust and remain open to change and new possibilities.

Education and Employment: Challenges and Achievements

My schooling experience had quite a precarious start. When I was three years old, my parents enrolled me in a preschool program for just two mornings a week, but after a few short weeks, they received a call from the teacher.

"The teacher suggested we take you out because you were very unhappy and couldn't adjust to the classroom environment," my mom recalled. "We tried a different preschool that was quieter but you were still unhappy."

Though I was unhappy, overwhelmed and agitated by what for me was constant sensory overload at both schools, I also sadly knew that I had failed but did not understand how or why.

"You have always strived for perfection," my mom attests. "It's just the way you were born; you have always applied it to everything."

In addition, my innate, unrelenting, literal mind and approach to everything only complicated things further.

"From kindergarten on," my mom remembers, "if a teacher said she was going to have test results or anything else by a certain day and it didn't happen, you would ask that teacher every day until it did."

Suffice it to say, I was never a favorite of my teachers, and I knew it. This led to more confusion and insecurity because I didn't understand why they thought I was such a problem and annoyance.

"Your need for constant reassurance and to do things perfectly," my mom continued, "was unrelenting. You always thought someone was mad at you, and you couldn't get past it. If I or anyone else raised their voice to you or showed annoyance, you were devastated; it was more than being sensitive."

Unfortunately, this has been a common theme throughout my life and something that I have not been able to fully overcome. I believe that with my innate literal mindset and inability to understand, process and cope with change along with essentially having been told that my ways of doing things and thought processes were wrong from such a young age for so many years, I was left with deeply ingrained feelings of fright, confusion and insecurity. I have done my best over the years to unapologetically be the best "me" possible, but am still sensitive to the opinions and reactions of others and never feel I am or have done well enough with anything, as I continually struggle with self-confidence and my need to be perfect and please everyone.

Despite it all and perhaps because of my need to make everyone happy and do what I knew was expected of me, I doggedly worked my way through my K-12 education, earning As and Bs along the way. And though my education was sidetracked and untraditional the years that I was institutionalized, I managed to catch up academically without too much problem upon returning to public school.

My dad inspired my love of many sports, including baseball.

Extracurricular activities helped me to adjust and remain under the radar. My lifelong enjoyment of sports and being active, especially outdoors, has always given me a sense of peace, so I found my way onto my high school's tennis and softball teams and eventually matriculated over to track and cross-country.

Finding my way onto the high school track team helped me to adjust and transition back to public school after being in the institution.

Though I have never been naturally talented at anything, my persistence and willingness to work and work hard has allowed me to achieve moderate successes throughout my school years and life in general.

Berkley High School graduation with Mom, 1989

Though I was forever an outsider, I think that my teammates had some respect for my unrelenting efforts to contribute to our team success which allowed me to make some acquaintances if not any real close or lifelong friends.

My diligence earned me a high enough grade point average to be eligible for college, and though I sometimes wonder if learning a trade might have been a better fit for me knowing what I do now, I am incredibly privileged and grateful to be blessed with supportive parents who saved and made it their priority to pay for my college degree at the University of Michigan in Ann Arbor where I earned a Bachelor of Science in Kinesiology and a K-12 teaching certificate.

Though I began my college experience in U of M's expansive Literature, Science and Arts School, I eventually found my way to their School of Kinesiology which was smaller and at the time had just three programs and choices of major: Movement Science, Sports Management and Communications and Physical Education. Students who chose to major in Physical Education were also required to earn a teaching certificate.

Early on in my studies, I was fortunate to have a very gentle and kind teacher who took a bit of an interest in me. After some time during a field work assignment that required us to work with elementary school children, putting them through various drills and tests, my teacher complimented my efforts and went so far as to say, "You should be a teacher!"

Add to this new phenomenon of someone actually voicing confidence in me, the fact that I have always wanted to help people and never wanted anyone to be made to feel the way that most teachers and many others made me feel, I was sold.

Mom, Dad, Michelle and me celebrating my graduation from University of Michigan in 1993.

Not long after this much needed endorsement, I officially declared my major to be Physical Education with the supplementary teaching certificate and graduated in 1993.

My employment history is long. I have been employed as a teacher in schools and private homes as well as in my work overseas in a variety of settings as a Peace Corps Volunteer. I have worked in running specialty stores and also became a freelance writer and published author.

I have worked in warehouses, grocery stores and many other fields in my efforts to put the needs of others first and earn a living and will forever continue to do so. I am a "jack of all trades" but am honest and work hard day in and out allowing me to look myself in the mirror each day despite my lack of confidence and desire to be better.

And while I have never been fired from a job, social barriers and confusion seem to remain a common theme no matter the situation, despite my efforts to continually learn the social rules and etiquette of our largely neurotypical-dominated world.

But no matter the challenges, I will continue to try to learn, be productive, help others and be the best person I can be, day in and out, while continuing to reinvent myself as life dictates.

Local Author Day at the 67th Annual Jewish Book Fair. I was chosen to speak on my newly-published book, *Six-Word Lessons on the Sport of Running*.

As a Peace Corps Volunteer, the Van Ster family welcomed me into their home and hearts; my love and gratitude for them is never-ending.

My little sister, Mercy (standing next to me on the right) loved to braid my hair!

A Namibian home in the desert, not far from the community where I worked and lived.

My Journey to Diagnosis

In 2000, after working in Texas for about a year, I returned to my home state of Michigan to begin a new job as a live-in teacher/nanny. Though I would be working with the family's two children, I was hired most specifically to work with the young boy who was experiencing a number of challenges. Though not formally diagnosed, professionals suspected him to have Asperger syndrome.

I had never heard of Asperger syndrome and the boy's parents were only beginning to learn what it was and how their son might be affected. Continuing to learn has always been important to me and so that is what I did; we found a teacher's conference for me to attend with a session specifically on Asperger syndrome.

Imagine my surprise when I arrived bright and early prepared to learn information relevant to helping my new charge, and instead, or perhaps in addition to, the instructor started describing me! Though we had never met, he seemed to know and understand me better than anyone, including myself. He explained things for which I had always been criticized. He validated my ways of doing things and gave reasons for why and how such methods were beneficial for me. He talked about many of my triggers, and described how and why things that are routine and normal for most would agitate me.

This experience, essentially from the moment he began speaking, was so insightful, validating and cathartic, I began to cry uncontrollably. This seemingly simple act of crying was monumental for me; I have never been an outwardly emotional person and am rarely physically able to cry despite often feeling the need.

After the session, despite my embarrassment as tears continued to stream down my face, I approached the instructor. I explained how it was like he customized his lecture to specifically talk about me. I explained how he understood and accepted things about me that my family did not. I explained how he essentially justified my whole life-- the struggles, the confusion, the often misplaced and inappropriate reactions--and I explained how I did not know why I was crying especially when I rarely did, but nonetheless could not stop. He listened patiently without judgment and waited until I was finished, then with kind, gentle, reassuring words, he explained that this was normal in his experience and that he had seen it happen in the past. Because my reaction was so strong, he encouraged me to learn more about Asperger syndrome and to consider seeking a diagnosis if after learning more, I still felt as strongly. He got me started with recommendations of authors to read, videos to watch and more lectures to attend.

I thanked him profusely and got on my way. I vividly remember pulling out my phone on my walk to my car, and with tears continuing to stream down my face, I announced to my mom as she answered the phone, "I think I have Asperger syndrome!" I was thirty years old.

It was a bit of a process to find and work through the information on Asperger syndrome which was fairly minimal and not widely known or sought at that time. But once I started, I could not get enough, as I craved the validation and illuminating justifications provided.

After reading the likes of Dr. Tony Attwood and Liane Holliday Willey, I asked my parents to review some of the information as well. My mom, ever the supporter, delved in immediately. Finding herself convinced and fascinated, she succeeded, after continual prodding, to convince my father, ever the cynic, to take a look for himself. As my dad is not much of a reader unless it has to do with sports or finances, I was especially grateful to learn that Dr. Attwood had videos that my dad made the time to watch with my mom.

One video was all it took. Everything hit home. The confusion, frustrations and battles we experienced over the years started to make sense. The information presented by Dr. Attwood explained me and provided reasons for my life history and so many things that were long misunderstood.

After receiving my father's validation, I was even more determined to learn if in fact I was born on the autism spectrum, and if there were reasons beyond my control for my being so different and challenged versus being stupid and difficult as I had been made to feel my whole life.

My path to diagnosis was not an easy one. Though I craved official validation, I was afraid of the alternative as well as the potential of actually having a disability and the baggage that could come with it.

Once I finally found the courage and strength to move forward, with the help of our local autism society, I contacted a psychologist they recommended. Unfortunately, I, and apparently those who gave the referral, were unaware that not all doctors are schooled in the different techniques and tools needed to evaluate an adult woman as opposed to a young male child for an autism diagnosis.

It ended up being an extremely humiliating and painful experience. Not only did the doctor use the same method one might employ for diagnosing children, he was very condescending and rude to my parents and me.

During our final session when he presented his findings, he concluded, "Well, you have something, but I don't know what it is."

There were no recommendations made or referrals given. I was left to continue coping on my own and made to feel as though I was weak and strange, someone who the doctor felt was just looking for excuses, though nothing could have been further from the truth.

Devastated, I did what I knew I had to do and have always done; I picked myself up and continued on as best as I could, trying to put the idea of autism to rest.

Fast forward nine years. I had never quite succeeded in losing my suspicion that everything I learned about autism explained me and my life, when I attended a conference that featured Dr. Tony Attwood.

For someone so accomplished and in demand, never have I met someone as kind, patient and humble as Dr. Attwood.

Though my tears began to flow uncontrollably once again after he began his presentation, I approached him during a break. He listened to my story, understood my emotional tears and explained that not all professionals understood that males and females exhibit symptoms differently, especially once they are adults who for years have had to try to learn and adapt. He explained that in order to receive a proper diagnosis or not, I needed to see a professional who was skilled in specifically understanding females and adults.

Though he did not know of anyone qualified in Michigan, he was able to recommend licensed psychologist Karen McKibbin, Psy.D. of Portland, Oregon.

I did search for a qualified candidate closer to home, but after coming up empty, I decided that I needed an answer once and for all.

With the support of my mom, I contacted Dr. McKibbin and we proceeded to fill out and send the information she needed that could be completed from home prior to our flight to Oregon for a series of meetings with her.

I remember my butterflies the morning that Dr. McKibbin would give us the results knowing there were different implications for whatever her findings turned out to be.

There was some relief when Dr. McKibbin diagnosed me to be on the autism spectrum, specifically with Asperger syndrome in conjunction with generalized anxiety disorder, but after leaving her warming, supportive presence, that relief was quickly accompanied by fear and doubt. The reactions of my father and sister when we called to let them know the results did not help; the hurt is still raw as I remember them saying, "Great! Now how do we fix you?"

There was additional letdown as the diagnosis did not reveal a magic plan to "fix me," make life instantly better or eliminate the pain and confusion that I have lived with for so long. But knowledge truly is power in my opinion and experience. Though I am a constant work in progress, knowing has helped me to make better decisions in my own best interest, and be a bit easier on myself when I can find the strength. I simply have a better understanding of who I am, why I do and need things a certain way and why some situations are so hard despite my best attempts to prevail and be "normal."

The decision to obtain a diagnosis is a very personal choice, but I do know that it was the right decision for me and can have many benefits.

My diagnosis led me to become an author and meet my publishers, Lonnie and Patty Pacelli. I am so grateful and proud to have earned their support and friendship.

Whether or not an individual seeks an official diagnosis, continuing to learn and believing in oneself is essential. This is a continual challenge for me but is something I work on regularly, and that is something to hold on to in and of itself.

My Top Six Challenges

Why six? As I prepared to share my primary life challenges, I was at a loss of where to begin. After contemplating long and hard, I chose challenges that I am never without and that make it particularly difficult for me to interact with or even be in the vicinity of people. These challenges also make it very difficult to function in the world at large. It is important to note that these difficulties can vary in intensity from day to day without any identifiable reason. It takes immense focus, determination and energy to conceal my struggles as I navigate the day, but I only allow myself to let go and decompress in private at the very end of the day when my responsibilities are complete. The time it takes for me to fully decompress can vary but is generally proportional to stressors faced throughout the day, coupled with the time it takes to develop a vivid, strategic plan for coping with the next day. The first five challenges listed greatly contribute to my number one challenge of all. They are counted down here:

6. Smells

Being overly sensitive to smells, I am bombarded daily with the natural and sometimes foul body orders of people, as well as any added scents including colognes, perfumes and shampoos. For me, these smells are overpowering and cause me to feel dizzy and agitated. In addition, there are countless other consuming smells in the environment, including cooking odors from restaurants and neighbors' homes, the stink of garbage, especially on trash pick-up day, and the stench of cigarette smoke, to name a few.

While not all smells are bothersome for me, including some particularly wonderful scents like the smell of rain or the changing of seasons or freshly baked bread, the unknown of what my olfactory system will be subject to at any given time is extremely unsettling as is the level of my sensitivity, which can vary from day to day without any apparent reason.

5. Sounds

Bailey Kennedy, my Labrador retriever, and I walked the 2013 Mutt March benefitting the Michigan Humane Society. Incredibly social, Bailey exhausts my sensory stamina but my love for her and her extreme enjoyment are worth every effort and are the reasons I take her to as many of these charitable events as possible.

I often consider myself more canine than human. I am loyal, forgiving and loving, though I am more similar to an Irish wolfhound than Labrador retriever in that I am reserved, independent, gentle in nature and have lots of quirks. Like most breeds though, I have a very keen sense of hearing; unfortunately, the disadvantages that come with it are many.

Socially, it is one more way that I am a dud. Take music for instance. Many believe, "the louder, the better." For me, the average volume that music is played is troublesome at best, so once it's cranked up, my pain becomes intolerable. Music that is broadcast throughout many stores is intimidating, especially knowing it will unavoidably be mixed with the ringing of phones and cash registers, people's conversations and the whirring of fans, air conditioners, heating systems and all the other sounds associated with running a business and being human. The self-control it takes for me to not fly off the handle is complicated and exhausting. I have heard many people express that they cannot live without music and find silence to be eerie. For me, any relative quiet is blissful but far from silent. There are still countless other sounds in any given environment including the revving of vehicle engines, the shrieking of children, the clatter of dishes and when I am lucky, the more pleasant

Who needs music when we have the beautiful all-consuming sounds of the forest? Nature offers my perfect type of music.

sounds such as the chatter of birds, the whoosh of the wind and the patter of rain.

4. Literal-mindedness

Only time and experience have taught me that people and life in general are not exactly as they seem. Despite having learned this, especially when unfamiliar with a situation or person, I still get blindsided.

A meeting scheduled for 2:00 pm often will not start exactly at 2:00 pm and sometimes will not happen at all. If someone says they will phone, I now know that they are likely just being polite and that I may not hear from them at all. If asked, "How are you doing?" I try to remember that this is more a figure of speech than someone actually wishing to know how I am feeling and what is going on in my life. If a store sign says that the business will open at 10:00 am, I realize now that they might not open at the designated time for any number of reasons. If there are big, dark, grey clouds in the sky, this does not always mean that it will rain even if the forecast is for 100 percent rain showers. The examples are endless.

I spent many years getting angry, frustrated, confused and truly devastated, most notably as to why people willingly mislead rather than being truthful. Though it still baffles me, I try to accept and expect this manner of people but choose not to do the same. I say what I mean and mean what I say. While it is never my intention to hurt anyone's feelings, I try to learn from past mistakes and be more tactful in my approach, but am never insincere.

My literal mind also causes me to miss or not understand jokes, metaphors and sarcasm, often making me a social pariah. No one wants to explain a joke or figure of speech, and people can quickly become annoyed feeling I have turned a lighthearted moment into a serious, complicated discussion when I truly only wish to understand.

Regrettably, the knowledge that I cannot believe much of what I see, hear and am told contributes to my mistrust, leaving me to feel sad, isolated and less inclined to interact with others and venture out. However, I continually try to reset and recharge despite my fears and hesitations.

3. Touch

For as long as I can remember, I have been over-sensitive to touch. For instance, my clothing needs to be exceptionally

I loved this socially appropriate loose-fitting dress and have learned to dress creatively versus the more confining, itchy styles required in my youth.

baggy and soft. If it is too close or rough, it will leave me feeling claustrophobic, pained, unable to focus, and I unconsciously will pull at it in an effort to rid myself of my discomfort.

Human touch is by far the most complicated. How do I realistically explain without hurting another's feelings that their physical touch, whether a hug, kiss or even anticipated stroke, is threatening and that my cringe is not intentional or a reflection of my feelings towards them? How do I convince people that as much as I would like to welcome their touch, it causes my body great pain and overwhelms my core? How do I explain that the deepest of pressure soothes my body and soul, but light contact makes me incredibly uncomfortable? How do I convince people that I ache to be normal and yearn with all my heart to have the ability to give and receive physical affection in the most traditional of ways? How do I properly explain that I very much need affection but must give and receive it in untraditional ways? How do I explain the guilt I feel for this very complicated and confusing ordeal?

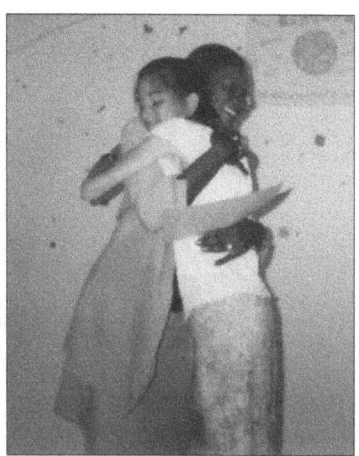

I genuinely accept affection whenever I can manage, as naturally as possible. The benefits are always worth the effort and any distress it may cause for me.

2. Change

It has taken many years for me to realize that the only constant in our world is change, often unexpected in nature. Also, permanence really does not exist for objects, ideas, relationships or much of anything. I still find myself taken aback when a product I use is altered or discontinued or needs to be replaced whether it no longer works, cannot be fixed or is simply outdated; or a married couple decides to divorce; or it becomes the norm to read books on a screen.

As a child, I had no concept of change. Every time it happened, which was often, I felt devastated, upset, angry and confused no matter how minute the change might be. Whether there was a new teacher at school, an unexpected visitor at my home, or dinner was not ready at the promised time, I would involuntarily fall apart. Even as I matured, the effects of change and my reactions as well as the time it took to adjust, were not much better, and while being informed in advance proved helpful, the negative effects on my initial reactions were constant.

Now just shy of completing my fifth decade, I reluctantly admit that while I now understand that change is a part of life, the effects and my initial response, especially when the change is unexpected and without advance notice, are only marginally improved. I cannot control how change makes me feel but believe I am more skilled in hiding my reactions and making plans to better cope, and I most certainly work on this daily.

1. Social Skills

The complexity of social skills is missed by many people who acquire these skills naturally and easily; this is not the case for people on the autism spectrum. In addition to the sarcasm and metaphors often used, the meaning of what is being conveyed is often implied rather than explicitly stated. Being very literal, I often fail to detect all that is meant and also have trouble with nonverbal forms of communication, including body language, touch and facial expressions.

Complicating matters further is my social endurance. I can run for hours and hours, but interacting with people overwhelms, exhausts and confuses me very quickly. In turn, especially if it is necessary for me to push beyond my limit which is most often the case, I end up feeling very ornery, sad and lonely. Unfortunately, at least for me, what qualifies as a social event or interaction is not limited to parties or a meal out with friends at a restaurant. Interactions at work, the store or home, even with family, are social; basic phone conversations with anyone are social; taking my dog for a walk and responding to impromptu friendly gestures requiring eye contact or simple conversations of well-intentioned people encountered along the way is social. While I am appreciative of any sincere social gesture or invitation and would like to accept them all, because I get socially fatigued so easily and often start the day that way, I try to limit my social availability for fear of being irritable or inappropriate due to my fatigue as well as my fear of making social blunders. Unfortunately, this can make me appear cold and distant when I am anything but, even if I need to show my appreciation, warmth and kindness in a different way.

Running: My Heart and Soul

I have always been a physically active person, consistently finding contentment when exerting myself, especially outdoors. Even as a young child, I was most at peace while riding my bike, playing catch or even shooting baskets long before I developed the strength and ability to put the ball through the hoop.

Because of my literal mindset and relentless desire to please, I worked hard to excel at the sports which were introduced to me by my dad and which met his approval. Running as a sport was not one of them; it was something you did while playing tee-ball or basketball. Forever naïve, I had no knowledge that running existed as a sport all on its own.

While my experience in the institution is something that still gives me nightmares, ironically this is where I first learned that running as a sport exists all on its own. I will never forget my first run. My lungs burned, my heart raced and while I do not remember how far or long I got to go, I do remember the freedom, peace and joy I felt like nothing I had ever experienced. Though I was not given the opportunity to run often during my time at the institution, I never turned down an opportunity and cherished this newfound discovery.

Once I was eventually released and returned to public schooling, I found my way onto my high school's track and cross-country teams. Though I have never been a phenomenal athlete, I did achieve moderate success as a long-distance runner, helping my teams to win meets. I earned my varsity letter in both track and cross-country. Additionally, my efforts, achievements and gentle nature secured the respect if not full acceptance of some of my teammates and allowed me to partially infiltrate their social circle. I teetered on the edge, but being on the outskirts still trumped complete outcast and also helped to further hide the red flags of my autism.

After graduating from high school, I continued my running and ventured into longer distances including marathons (26.2 miles) and ultramarathons (longer than 26.2 miles). To date, I have completed a total of 77 races of marathon distance or longer, including three 100-mile races and two Boston Marathons.

With just over two minutes to spare, I was ecstatic to qualify for the 100th running of the Boston Marathon at the 1995 Detroit Free Press Marathon.

I also dabble in multisports, including triathlons and duathlons, and run many shorter races of varying lengths each year throughout the seasons, including snowshoe races in the winter.

Greg Sadler Photography

I enjoy every distance, short or long. I love to take on new challenges and have no intentions of ever quitting the sport.

The pleasure I get from running and racing has become complex. First and foremost, I find joy in the movement itself and love to experience a variety of outdoor surfaces, single track trail being my favorite. Running is how I begin my day, no matter how early I have to wake as I find that it gives me the strength and stamina to face the many challenges that I will inevitably encounter throughout the day.

Running also provides my life with excitement, challenge and discovery as well as a welcome if daunting and previously unforeseen social element. While I mostly prefer to train on my own, allowing for peace and solitude that are otherwise largely absent throughout the course of any given day, races are a whole 'nother animal. As grateful as I am for the people I have met and friends I have made, it takes a great deal of energy and courage to go to the races, because they present many social challenges.

When I first started attending races, just being in the presence of others was as much as I could manage. I would warm up for the race, hide in my car until the race began, and leave shortly after the results were announced. Eventually I managed to make eye contact with a few kind souls which led to brief greetings and short conversations.

With my longtime friend, Bill, just before the start of a 100K trail race.

I'm not fast but give my all at every race – 5Ks are tough too!

In 2013, in honor of my mom, in the fight against breast cancer, I proudly walked 60 miles and raised more than $2,000 at the Susan G. Komen 3-Day for the Cure.

I have always been a creature of habit, and my continued presence was noticed and welcomed despite all my quirks. My nerves persist, and I generally still hide in my car until it's time to line up for the start of the race. I always try to be friendly to everyone and find that I can socialize a bit better and longer after I finish the race when my natural endorphins have kicked in.

My meltdowns come later, very intentionally in private. I replay in my mind every interaction and make a plan to correct and apologize for any mistakes I believe I have made.

To date, I have raced in nineteen different states, four countries, two continents and countless communities I never knew existed, even in my home state, each with its own unique beauty and character. The people I have met, the adventures had, and the splendor seen far outweigh the social and sensory difficulties that persist and are why, despite my continual inclination to stay home and run on my own, I force myself to cope and enjoy the privilege of so many wonderful experiences.

During a scheduled vacation during my Peace Corps service, I took a 23-hour bus ride from Namibia to South Africa to run the Old Mutual Two Oceans 56K race (my first ultramarathon) which they call "The World's Most Beautiful Marathon." It was beautiful and challenging, even as it poured pretty much the entire race.

Running has also provided professional opportunities, including my start as a writer. It was during my service as a Peace Corps Volunteer in Namibia that I ventured to write an article about a running and racing experience for some of my learners. My intention was to highlight some of this lesser-known developing country's needs. Through a running acquaintance, I contacted the editor of the oft-read *Michigan Runner* magazine. My article was published, and they kept me on as a freelance journalist for over twelve years until they discontinued their print edition in 2016.

My running also helps me to travel, cope with change and uncertainty and provide some structure even to days that are vastly unknown. Wherever I go, my running shoes accompany me without fail, allowing me to continue my morning routine even if I am limited to running loops in a parking lot versus a more preferred route.

Like a treasured spouse, I try daily not to take my running for granted. I am diligent about doing the homework necessary to avoid injury. I consistently make sure that I have proper shoes, engage in strength work and cross training and keep a positive, grateful attitude as I never wish to lose "my better half."

Final Thoughts

"What do you want to be when you grow up?" A common question posed to wide-eyed youth by well-intentioned adults.

Many children have ambitious, creative responses to such a question and lofty dreams for the future; I have always come up empty. So much of my time and energy are spent navigating each over-stimulating, confusing day that planning for the future gets lost in the process. Being very literal complicates matters further. It's hard to envision something so unknown, and it has always been very difficult to muster the confidence to believe that I would be wanted or even good for doing much of anything.

Simply and truthfully naïve, all I have ever wanted is to help people and to be loved and liked.

Though I continually get absorbed in details and struggle with self-confidence, I have over the years surprised myself.

My life is far from traditional, but I am proud of my moral compass, my ability to stand strong and make decisions, often difficult in nature, on issues that matter most and to differ from the mainstream when needed, which for better or worse is often. I take pride in never giving up, even when I fall, never allowing myself to stay down for too long before I force myself to get back up and move on.

"Less is more" is one of my favorite mottos and very relevant to my own life and ways of doing things. I am far from popular but grateful for my genuine friends and family. I have never married, but am thankful for many of the romantic relationships I have experienced, and while skeptical of ever finding a forever partner for myself, I remain open to the idea. I do not have children but have had the most wonderful animals in my life, including my precious twelve-year-old Labrador retriever, Bailey Kennedy. My career path is highly unconventional, but I am proud of the accomplishments I have made, people I have helped and my nonnegotiable resolve to always give my best and put my family first as needed and as increased health challenges have dictated in recent years.

From a scared, confused, insecure child, never would I have dreamed to publish one book let alone three; to have genuine friends and family who actually like, love and respect me despite my quirks and doubts; to genuinely help and teach people if even in small numbers and untraditional methods; to achieve athletic challenges; and to meet the great, late, Hockey Hall of Fame icon, Ted Lindsay, whose charitable autism research foundation chose me to receive the 2017 Individual Courage Award for living courageously with an autism spectrum disorder.

Accepting the Courage Award from the Ted Lindsay Foundation
Carrie Hall Photography

Courage Award ceremony with Ted Lindsay and my parents, 2017
Carrie Hall Photography

After taking the time to read my story, my hope is that you will benefit from the information I have shared, lessons I have learned, and mottos that I do my best to live by, including:

- Never give up and believe in yourself no matter the opinion of others.

- Life may not be as it seems, but it is full of wonderful people and opportunities just waiting to be found and explored.

- Mistakes do not equal failure; they are an important way to learn, grow and become stronger and braver.

- The willingness to ask for and accept help is a sign of strength, not weakness.

- There is no one right way to live; only the manner that works best for each individual.

- Change is incredibly hard and scary but is often necessary, healthier than the alternative and can lead to better things.

- Never say never. We can all make achievements we might never have imagined, thought possible or even considered.

- There are many different types of intelligences, one no better than the other; we need them all to keep our world functioning and interesting.

- Never assume.

- Own and learn from mistakes, correct when possible, apologize when relevant and move forward.

- Never stop learning; it is impossible for anyone to know everything.

- Never minimize the challenges of others.

- Never underestimate yourself or anyone else.

- Do things that are difficult; often the benefits far outweigh the hardships.

- Allow others to make mistakes; do not hold grudges.

- Treat others the way you wish to be treated; we do not have to like everyone, but it is essential to be kind and courteous to one and all.

- It is OK to not be perfect; no one is.

- Different does not equal wrong.

- Compromise is essential.

As I continue along the bumpy, unpredictable road of life, I will continually strive to learn, to be a better person, to make positive differences in our world, and to apologize for and correct mistakes I will inevitably make along the way. I find that life is very much akin to the amusement roller coaster rides that I fear and seek all at once, but inevitably enjoy, and isn't that in part what life is all about?

Aimee and I met as freshmen at the University of Michigan and have been friends ever since.

My mom, my biggest supporter, got up long before dawn to see me off as I began my 60-mile trek in support of her and the fight for a cure to end breast cancer.

At every stage of life, no matter our many battles and conflicts, my parents have supported me, unconditionally.

My first date--high school Homecoming Dance, sophomore year

A particularly cold February parkrun race. Sub-zero temperatures do not deter me!

Winter Spring, Summer, Fall, I truly love to run through it all!

Named after my maternal grandfather, my bunny Joe, was sweet, smart and playful (May 1998 - June 2008).

Mollie and Joe, the best of friends

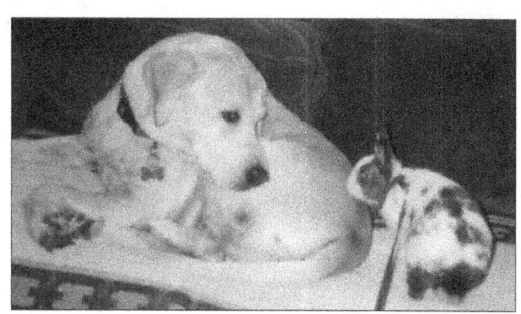

My loving (and truly patient), Samantha

Me and sweet Roxanne

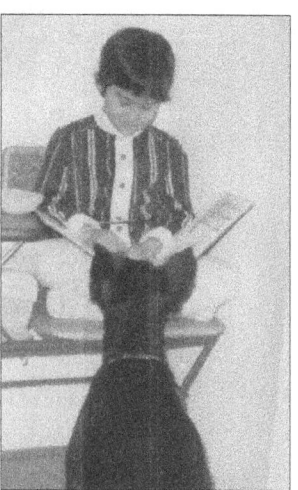

Dandy was loyal and sweet, even when I didn't have pretzels (hidden in my lap) to share!

Best Practices for People with Autism

Volunteer

In addition to helping people, animals, the environment and any number of worthy organizations, volunteering can lead to valuable networking, employment and social opportunities. Volunteers often learn new skills and are incredibly important and appreciated. Some volunteer work requires a commitment, but there are many opportunities to volunteer occasionally, in ways that work best for individual schedules and preferences. Some volunteer work does not even require leaving home. Operation Gratitude (*OperationGratitude.com*) has a letter writing campaign to express appreciation to deployed troops, first responders, and emergency medical personnel.

Call or explore the websites of organizations in which you have a vested interest. Idealist is a nonprofit organization that connects people and organizations. On their website, *Idealist.org*, you can search for opportunities by location, interest and skill. Stay connected to favorite organizations by signing up to receive their e-newsletters for opportunities. Possibilities are endless, and I have experienced more pleasant surprises than I ever could have imagined or thought possible through volunteering.

I can be found many a Saturday running and volunteering with my Livonia parkrun friends, wearing shirts we earned by volunteering 25 times.

Challenge Yourself

Life is hard, and we all make mistakes, get disappointed and feel down and discouraged at times. It is OK and beneficial to allow time for feeling sad and to take breaks in order to reenergize. However, it is also essential to not wallow in self-pity. I try to challenge myself daily, forcing myself to do things that are hard and uncomfortable whether it is going to the grocery store or deviating from my valued routine in order to help someone or take part in a social situation. It could be making necessary but daunting life changes or signing up for and running a 100-mile race, which I enjoy, but also comes with a great deal of difficulties and unknowns.

Keep in mind that it doesn't matter how big or small the challenge is or if what is hard for you is easy for someone else. We all have assets and weaknesses, but if we don't put ourselves out there, we minimize our abilities to learn and connect, to keep life interesting and to find happiness.

In 1993, I independently signed up with American Youth Hostels, Inc. for a three-week backpacking trip to Alaska. Despite my fears, it was an incredibly fun trip and I even got to hike on glaciers!

I love and believe in the quote from one of my favorite movies, the 1992 sports comedy film, *A League of Their Own*, where the character Jimmy Dugan, played by Tom Hanks, says, "It's supposed to be hard. If it wasn't hard, everyone would do it. The hard . . . is what makes it great."

Note from the Author

Thank you for reading my story and I hope it has been helpful for you or anyone in your life connected to autism.

I would love to hear your thoughts and I am available for speaking engagements and other appearances. I wish to help as many individuals as possible to have better lives.

You can reach me at Tracey@GrowingUpAutistic.com

Learn more about my books, articles and interviews at GrowingUpAutistic.com/Tracey

Recommended Resources

Organizations and Websites

Jessica Kingsley Publishers, *JKP.com*

> According to the website, "Jessica Kingsley Publishers publishes books pertaining to the social sciences and behavioral sciences, with special attention to art therapy and autism spectrum disorders, respectively." They are a good source to search for new autism spectrum disorder related works and favored authors.

Autism Society, *Autism-Society.org*

National Autism Association, *NationalAutismAssociation.org*

> Staying connected with the growing wealth of new autism information and resources is essential and can be overwhelming. To start, I recommend getting and staying connected with your local autism society. Both of these organizations can help connect people to their local autism societies and providers and also offer a great deal of relevant updated information, programs and more.

parkrun, *parkrun.com*

This running organization is a collection of 5-kilometer (3.1 mi) running/walking events that take place every Saturday morning throughout the United States and abroad. All parkrun events are free and are managed by local volunteers. These events are incredibly inclusive and welcoming to everyone whether a person wishes to run, walk, volunteer or just be there to watch and support the other participants. All events have an optional meeting place, generally a nearby coffee shop, for people to socialize after the run/walk. No prior commitment is required to attend. Some communities have begun a 2-kilometer "junior parkrun" specifically for kids on Sundays, but children are welcome and encouraged to attend on Saturdays with an adult, and no one is obligated to complete the entire 5K distance. While not all countries or communities have a parkrun, more are being added regularly, and the website contains information for those who wish to start their own event.

Books

Liane Holliday Willey, *Pretending to Be Normal: Living with Asperger's Syndrome*, Jessica Kingsley Publishers (Expanded Edition) 2014. *Aspie.com*

This was one of the very first books I read after learning about autism spectrum disorder. Though it took nine years for me to receive an official diagnosis, this book very much reflected my own life and absolutely validated my feelings and pursuit of an answer. Liane is a wonderful writer and speaker whom I highly recommend.

Tony Attwood, *The Complete Guide to Asperger's Syndrome*, Jessica Kingsley Publishers, 2008. *TonyAttwood.com.au*

A treasure trove of valuable information, the video version leaving my father with no doubts as to whether I was born on the autism spectrum. Attwood too is an incredibly talented writer and charismatic speaker whose works I fully recommend and delve into as often as possible.

Karen McKibbin, *Life on the Autism Spectrum: A Guide for Girls and Women*, Jessica Kingsley Publishers, 2015.

Another must-read to better understand females and why we often stay under the radar preventing us from receiving much needed support.

Trevor Pacelli, *Six-Word Lessons on Growing Up Autistic: 100 Lessons to Understand How Autistic People See Life.* Pacelli Publishing, 2012. *GrowingUpAutistic.com*

Patty Pacelli, *Six-Word Lessons for Autism-Friendly Workplaces: 100 Lessons for Employers and Employees to Succeed Together.* Pacelli Publishing, 2014. *GrowingUpAutistic.com*

Lonnie Pacelli, *Six-Word Lessons for Dads with Autistic Kids: 100 Lessons to Help Fathers and their Children Create Strong Bonds.* Pacelli Publishing, 2013. *GrowingUpAutistic.com*

Tracey Cohen, *Six Word Lessons on Female Asperger Syndrome: 100 Lessons to Understand and Support Girls and Women with Asperger's*. Pacelli Publishing, 2015. *GrowingUpAutistic.com/Tracey*

> I humbly wish to recommend my own book as I worked hard to create a very concise resource applicable to all ages, genders, intellects, experience levels and attention spans. Each succinct lesson contains a wealth of information and can be read sequentially as well as stand on its own. Lessons can be aptly revisited for assurance, reminders, the various stages of life and more.

www.ingramcontent.com/pod-product-compliance
Lightning Source LLC
Chambersburg PA
CBHW070655050426
42451CB00008B/370